DO WHAT YOU LIKE

JOBS IF YOU LIKE
Math

Stuart A. Kallen

San Diego, CA

About the Author

Stuart A. Kallen is the author of more than 350 nonfiction books for children and young adults. He has written on topics ranging from the theory of relativity to the art of electronic dance music. Kallen won a Green Earth Book Award from the Nature Generation environmental organization for his book *Trashing the Planet: Examining the Global Garbage Glut*. In his spare time, he is a singer, songwriter, and guitarist in San Diego.

© 2025 ReferencePoint Press, Inc.
Printed in the United States

For more information, contact:
ReferencePoint Press, Inc.
PO Box 27779
San Diego, CA 92198
www.ReferencePointPress.com

ALL RIGHTS RESERVED.
No part of this work covered by the copyright hereon may be reproduced or used in any form or by any means—graphic, electronic, or mechanical, including photocopying, recording, taping, web distribution, or information storage retrieval systems—without the written permission of the publisher.

Picture Credits:
Cover: DC Studio/Shutterstock
 8: PeopleImages.com-Yuri A/Shutterstock
18: Gorodenkoff/Shutterstock
32: A.PAES/Shutterstock
42: Gorodenkoff/Shutterstock
51: NASA

LIBRARY OF CONGRESS CATALOGING-IN-PUBLICATION DATA

Names: Kallen, Stuart A., 1955- author.
Title: Jobs if you like math / by Stuart A. Kallen.
Description: San Diego, CA : ReferencePoint Press, Inc., 2025. | Series: Do what you like | Includes bibliographical references and index. | Audience term: Teenagers
Identifiers: LCCN 2024043962 (print) | LCCN 2024043963 (ebook) | ISBN 9781678209841 (library binding) | ISBN 9781678209858 (ebook)
Subjects: LCSH: Mathematics--Vocational guidance--Juvenile literature.
Classification: LCC QA10.5 .K35 2025 (print) | LCC QA10.5 (ebook) | DDC 510.23--dc23/eng/20240925
LC record available at https://lccn.loc.gov/2024043962
LC ebook record available at https://lccn.loc.gov/2024043963

Contents

Introduction: The Language of the Universe	4
Accountant	7
Data Scientist	15
Mathematician	23
Economist	31
Computer Information and Research Scientist	40
Physicist	49
Source Notes	57
Interview with a Physicist	59
Other Jobs If You Like Math	62
Index	63

Introduction:
The Language of the Universe

Sports lovers might not realize it, but they sometimes use advanced math concepts when analyzing the performance of their favorite teams. Sports analysts rely on probability theory, statical analysis, and percentages to rate players and predict game outcomes. Tim Zue turned his love of sports—and math—into a career as a sports analyst for the Boston Red Sox baseball team. Zue uses math concepts like tactical assessment, movement analysis, and statistical modeling to improve team performance. Zue describes his career path:

> I was a very passionate Boston sports fan growing up, and I have also always had a love for math, numbers, data, and information throughout my life. I was on the math team in high school and . . . when I found myself working as an unpaid summer intern for the Boston Red Sox [I] realized that I could combine my love of sports, data and analytics, and business into a single career . . . in sports analytics.[1]

Not everyone loves calculus, statistics, probability, and other types of math, but those who do can develop skills that are transferable to many types of jobs. Architects design buildings based on mathematical concepts, including calculus and advanced geometry. Carpenters, plumbers, electricians, masons, and other skilled workers need to understand everything from fractions to trigonometry when constructing buildings. Meteorologists who study weather patterns make forecasts using data science, statistical modeling, and physics. Physicians combine their problem-solving skills with statistics and probability to determine the most effective treatments for patients.

Job Satisfaction in Math Fields

Doing math problems in a classroom might make some students cringe. But a 2021 study by researchers Pär Bjälkebring and Ellen Peters showed that people who have math-based careers have higher rates of job satisfaction and are generally happier than others. These conclusions are backed by the *U.S. News & World Report* article "The Best Jobs in America." Every year the magazine analyzes around two hundred jobs and rates them on criteria that include salary, unemployment rates, avenues for promotion, and other data. In 2024 a majority of the top ten best jobs in America were filled by professionals who were well versed in mathematics. The careers included financial manager, software developer, information technology manager, data scientist, and actuary.

People who understand math might be happier because they make more money than professionals in other fields. And you do not have to be a math genius to understand why math careers pay more. Experts in math are urgently needed in almost every job sector, including education, entertainment, finance, technology, health care, and space exploration. They are called on to conduct research, study statistics, analyze data, and develop the next generation of robotics, quantum computers, and artificial intelligence.

The Bureau of Labor Statistics (BLS) predicts the number of math-related jobs will grow by more than thirty-three thousand annually through 2030. Half the new jobs will be for data scientists, but there is also a growing need for statisticians, engineers, and research analysts. The high demand translates to high wages. According to the BLS, the annual median wage for math occupations was $101,460 in 2023, more than double the $48,060 median annual wage for all occupations.

Broader Applications of Math

Math skills help people think logically, analyze and solve problems, identify patterns, and pay close attention to detail, qualities that are useful in everyday life. Shoppers use addition, subtraction, and percentages to figure out savings, discounts, and sales tax. Cooks rely on measurements, fractions, and conversions when following recipes in the kitchen. And many studies have found that practicing math helps keep the brain healthy and improves thinking skills over time. A 2021 study by the International Commission on Mathematical Instruction shows that math "provides an effective way of building mental discipline and encourages logical reasoning and mental rigor. In addition, mathematical knowledge plays a crucial role in understanding the contents of other school subjects such as science, social studies, and even music and art."[2]

Studying mathematics might be difficult for some, but math provides a language that can help one understand this world and the universe beyond. As Italian astronomer and physicist Galileo Galilei wrote in the seventeenth century, "[The universe] cannot be read until we have learnt the language and become familiar with the characters in which it is written. It is written in mathematical language, and the letters are triangles, circles and other geometrical figures, without which means it is humanly impossible to comprehend."[3]

Accountant

What Does an Accountant Do?

Tracy Coenen believes that anyone who is charged with a crime is innocent until proved guilty. And she believes that defendants facing criminal charges deserve the best defense possible. But Coenen is not a lawyer. She is a forensic accountant. She uses her accounting skills to comb through extremely complex financial transactions made by people accused of money laundering, embezzlement, tax fraud, and other crimes. Coenen makes clear that her job is not about helping defendants escape punishment but ensuring that they are fairly charged and that the numbers used in their prosecutions are accurate. "The most important part of my job . . . is being honest with the numbers," says Coenen. "The numbers don't lie. The evidence is often very definitive, and it is up to me to report my findings accurately. It is never okay to lie or stretch the truth in the defense of an alleged criminal."[4]

Coenen says her job is both interesting and necessary. But most certified public accountants (CPAs) do not work with criminal defendants. Coenen writes, "CPAs often see themselves as financial watchdogs, especially when they are providing

---

A Few Facts

Typical Earnings
Median annual pay of $79,880 in 2023

Educational Requirements
Bachelor's degree, certification

Personal Qualities
Good math and communication skills, honest, analytical, detail-oriented

Work Settings
Full time in offices, with overtime when deadlines loom

Future Outlook
Growth of 4 percent through 2032

Accountants work with businesses, individuals, and government agencies. Their job is to make sure their clients follow all tax laws and financial regulations. They might also manage public funds or oversee an organization's finances.

traditional accounting or auditing services."[5] As watchdogs, accountants examine financial records, prepare tax returns, and make sure that required taxes are paid on time. Accountants also perform payroll services that include calculating employee work hours, making bank deposits, and writing paychecks. The job includes helping clients find low-risk investment opportunities and working with businesses to reduce costs and increase profits.

Accountants are often specialists. They work with businesses or individuals to confirm that these clients are following strict tax laws and financial regulations. Some accountants are employed by city, state, and federal government agencies. Government accountants might also manage public funds, investigate white-collar crime, and perform financial audits for agencies.

While various types of accountants do similar work, they may have differing responsibilities and titles. Large businesses and accounting firms employ management accountants to oversee all accounting and financial reporting in an organization. Sometimes referred to as comptrollers, these professionals prepare budgets and manage financial assets. They help companies make major business decisions and handle aspects of real estate and stock transactions.

CPAs might work with large and small businesses, government agencies, or individuals. Some, like Coenen, work as forensic accountants. What sets CPAs apart is that they have additional training and are licensed by a governing body called the Board of Accountancy, which holds them to a code of professional ethics. Accountants with a CPA license are credentialed to perform tasks such as auditing public companies and performing internal audits for government tax agencies such as the Internal Revenue Service. CPAs also create quarterly earnings reports for businesses and ensure that financial documents follow legal reporting standards.

A Typical Workday

The workday of an accountant depends on the type of work performed. Tax accountants might work alone in an office and deal with several different individuals with unique financial issues. Corporate and government accountants are often part of teams that focus on specific tasks such as budgeting or auditing. Whatever the specifics, most accountants start their days by checking and responding to emails, texts, and voicemails. They consult their schedules and prepare documents for meetings, writing down questions and discussion points. Many accountants closely follow the financial news media so they can quickly react to daily changes in the stock market, banking industry, and other financial sectors.

Bookkeeping and number crunching fill up an accountant's day. Like most accountants, CPA Ben Watson relies on the Microsoft Excel spreadsheet software to review and analyze financial data, record transactions, and prepare financial reports. He says, "[People] immediately think I must absolutely love math and I'm great with numbers. While I enjoy math, I still let Microsoft Excel do most of the heavy lifting."[6]

Software can take care of the basic math, which leaves time for accounting tasks such as providing financial advice for clients. Accountants are expected to help clients find legal ways to maximize profits and avoid overpaying taxes. This requires accountants to comb through the intricacies of tax codes and government regulations, both of which can change periodically. Accountants read industry articles and reports to ensure they are using accurate data and correct methods when they perform their jobs.

Much accounting work is driven by regular deadlines; accountant Alan Hester writes, "Typical work revolves around month-end close (closing the books each month), tax filing deadlines, quarterly financial updates, and year-end close (closing the books for the year), to name a few."[7]

Education and Training

Accountants usually have a bachelor's degree in accounting, finance, business, or a related field. Those who hope to work for large accounting firms can earn more by obtaining a master of business administration degree. In college, they may focus on specialized programs like forensic accounting, bookkeeping, auditing, or tax accounting.

Not all accounting jobs require certification, but those who become CPAs enhance their job and salary prospects. Each state has an agency called the Board of Accountancy that issues CPA certificates. All states require accountants to complete 150 semester hours of coursework, 30 more hours than required to attain a typical four-year bachelor's degree. Prospective CPAs are then required to pass a four-part test, called the Uniform CPA

Mistakes Can Be Costly

"Accounting is a deadline-driven job and accountants are known to work a lot of overtime when a deadline approaches. . . . It's important to keep in mind this is money that belongs to a person or company and not just a bunch of numbers. The worst thing to happen is to lose money on paper due to mistakes. Any miss-postings or wrong interpretation of the tax code can cost a business or a client thousands if not millions of dollars, including a loss of reputation for the accountant and the business."

—Alan Hester, corporate accountant

Alan Hester, "What Is an Accountant Day to Day Schedule Like?," Career Village, December 27, 2022. www.careervillage.org.

Examination, from the American Institute of Certified Public Accountants (AICPA). After certification is granted, it is compulsory for CPAs to take educational courses on a regular basis.

CPAs can obtain further accreditation from the AICPA to demonstrate their competence in specialized fields. Certifications include Accredited in Business Valuation, Certified in Financial Forensics, Certified Information Technology Professional, and Personal Financial Specialist.

The Association of Government Accountants offers the Certified Government Financial Manager for those who work in federal, state, or local government agencies. Other certifications are offered for specialists in internal auditing, management accounting, and international accounting.

Skills and Personality

Accounting relies on mathematics, and accountants need to have strong basic math skills along with a good knowledge of calculus and statistics. They commonly use advanced accounting software and therefore need to be proficient with computers.

New Projects Every Day

"I am currently a consultant for CFO Advisory [Services], which means that the company I work for places me on client projects. It's very rewarding because I know I am making a difference for the company. I gain friendships and share my knowledge and mentor others. No project is ever the same, which I do enjoy. I am able to work in different industries and performing a variety of accounting tasks, it's never the same day to day or project to project. If you're outgoing and like to meet different people, and learn different things, then consulting may be a fit for you."

—Angela Peterson, accounting consultant

Angela Peterson, "What Does an Accountant Do on a Typical Day?," Career Village, December 22, 2023. www.careervillage.org.

Accountants also need to be extremely detail oriented. They often deal with large sums of money and strict tax laws. A small error might cause a business serious financial harm. Misleading tax advice might even expose a client to a large fine or criminal charges. Accountants need to be aware of this and ensure absolute accuracy in all documents they prepare and advice they provide. This requires accountants to be honest, analytical, and organized.

Accountants manage sensitive financial data, which requires them to have a strong ethical foundation. They cannot discuss confidential information with others, and they need to take strict data security measures on computers to prevent leaks, hacks, and disclosures.

Translating accounting principles into useful information for clients requires accountants to possess effective communication skills. Because money is at stake, accountants must respond quickly and plainly to clients. CPA Logan Allec says communication is a major part of his job. "I have to write emails to clients on a daily basis explaining complex tax or accounting issues in language they can understand," he says. "I have to draft memos documenting tax positions. I have to write instructions to others on my team so they can do their jobs better."[8]

Working Conditions

Accountants who work for corporations, government agencies, and financial firms work in offices. CPAs, who mostly focus on keeping books and filing tax forms for individuals, might work out of a small office or a home office. Some travel to meet clients at their businesses, where company records are kept.

Bookkeeping requires accountants to review, document, and finalize all transactions at the end of each month and year. During this process, called month-end closing and year-end closing, respectively, accountants often work overtime. Tax accountants who prepare individual tax returns begin working long hours in January and continue through the tax filing deadline of April 15—and often several weeks beyond.

Employers and Earnings

Accountants work in many major economic sectors, including banking and financial services, real estate, health care, and insurance. They are also employed by large and small businesses of all types. Some work for local, state, and federal government agencies. Around 4 percent are self-employed.

According to the Bureau of Labor Statistics (BLS), around one quarter of all accountants work for accounting, payroll, tax preparation, and bookkeeping firms. Many are employed by what are called the Big Four accounting firms: Deloitte, Ernst & Young, Klynveld Peat Marwick Goerdeler, and PricewaterhouseCoopers. The Big Four perform about two-thirds of all accounting-related work worldwide and have over $200 billion in annual revenue.

The median annual pay for accountants in 2023 was $79,880, according to the BLS. Those employed by financial and insurance firms earned the highest median pay, $83,250. Accountants in the top 10 percent of earners brought in more than $137,280 annually.

Future Outlook

Businesses need to navigate the increasingly complex world of taxes, regulations, and finance to be successful. With a growing demand for professionals to prepare and examine financial records and handle the legal requirements of government agencies, the demand for accountants is predicted to increase by 4 percent through 2032, according to the BLS.

Find Out More

Accounting Today
www.accountingtoday.com
This site is an information resource for public accountants. It features blogs and news about the latest trends in professional accounting. Visitors to the site can find podcasts, webinars, and educational and career information.

American Institute of Certified Public Accountants (AICPA)
www.aicpa-cima.com
The AICPA is the national professional organization for certified public accountants in the United States. The organization provides study and learning tools for CPAs and administers the CPA exam. Visitors can take advantage of the website's career-development information, apprenticeship programs, and study options.

Association of Government Accountants (AGA)
www.agacgfm.org
The AGA is a professional organization for accountants who work for local, state, and federal governments. It offers certification, ethics guidelines, webinars, and continuing education tools to aspiring accountants.

Data Scientist

What Does a Data Scientist Do?

Data includes facts, information, and statistics related to anything and everything. In the digital world, data is created every time a text is sent, a movie is streamed, a meal is ordered, or a purchase is made online. With more than 5.4 billion active internet users worldwide in 2024, nearly 403 billion gigabytes of data are generated, captured, copied, and consumed each day, according to the online data-gathering platform Statista. This mind-boggling amount of generated data increases every year. And the information is a digital gold mine that drives the internet economy, which was worth $2.6 trillion in the United States in 2022.

Businesses and organizations that profit from the digital economy rely on data scientists to capture and study the massive streams of data created every day. Data scientists search for patterns in databases and analyze them to help companies make business decisions. Data scientist Diogo Ferreira explains, "A data scientist is a sort of a fortune teller that uses numbers to make predictions, studies and compares possible scenarios . . . and tries to find the possible causes for events that are being observed in the real world. A

A Few Facts

Typical Earnings
Median annual pay of $108,020 in 2023

Educational Requirements
Master's degree in data science, computer science, engineering, or mathematics

Personal Qualities
Strong science and math skills, business knowledge, good communicator

Work Settings
Full time in offices

Future Outlook
Growth of 35 percent through 2032

data scientist also studies ways of improving those predictions, or to better understand the reasons behind [whatever] is happening."[9]

To understand the job of a data scientist, it is helpful to look at an e-commerce site like Amazon, which is responsible for about 40 percent of all online sales in the United States. Amazon maintains vast databases filled with information on its customers that includes names, ages, phone numbers, addresses, credit card numbers, shopping histories, and even religious and political affiliations. Data scientists who work for Amazon study information about customer buying histories, product returns, seasonal purchases, and other factors. The retailer can use this data to time the release of new products and offer deals and sales. The data also predicts economic upturns and downturns and can help the company determine when to hire and fire employees.

Unlike data analysts, who pore over numbers and other bits of information to make predictions, data scientists use models or algorithms based on questions they or their employers deem important. Sometimes a model to answer the question exists, and a data scientist must know which will work to get the right results; sometimes the data scientist must create a model specific to the needs of the client.

These models and the data they produce are relevant beyond the sphere of business and profitmaking. Some data scientists, like Chris Holdgraf, use models to conduct medical research. In one experiment, Holdgraf collected data from electrodes placed directly on the surface of test subjects' skulls. Holdgraf created a computer program to analyze the data. This helped him learn how humans hear sounds and respond to them. There are hopes that this data can someday help people who are hearing impaired. As Holdgraf says, "Being a data scientist gives me the flexibility to work with people with many different kinds of backgrounds and to work on problems that are meaningful to lots of different communities, which I really enjoy."[10]

Unique People Wanted

"We often say we're looking for 'unicorns' to join our team, applied data scientists with the skills and interest to excel and bring innovation. . . . When we look for entry-level data scientists, more than anything else, we're looking for that curiosity and the ability to be a self-starter. If you're willing to soak up as much information as you can over your first few months, work consistently on your coding skills, and then dive into complicated, interdisciplinary problems, you might be a good fit for a data science team."

—Nick Resnick, data scientist

Nick Resnick, "Data Scientist: A Day in the Life," Enterprisers Project, September 15, 2022. www.enterprisersproject.com.

A Typical Workday

Most data scientists will agree that it is difficult to define an average workday. The job often involves identifying and solving big problems, and each day presents new challenges. Data scientist Sakshi Gupta says the main part of her job is analyzing the day's problem: "Data is only as good as the questions you ask. Unless a data scientist asks the right questions, [the data] cannot provide the right insights for better business decision-making. This involves various tasks such as understanding the business requirements, scoping an efficient solution, and planning the data analysis."[11] After defining the problem, the data scientist will collect raw data from client databases and elsewhere. This data might include information about sales and returns, purchase histories, customer feedback, market surveys, and users' website searches.

Data scientists often refer to raw data as "dirty" because it is usually unorganized, inaccurate, incomplete, irrelevant, or in the wrong format. Dirty data can trip up algorithms and create inaccurate results. That is why data scientists spend around 70 percent of their time in a process called data cleaning. This process

Businesses that profit from the digital economy rely on data scientists to capture and study the massive streams of data created every day. Data scientists search for patterns in databases and analyze them to help companies make business decisions.

involves detecting, correcting, and deleting inaccurate or irrelevant information. Most data scientists say this is the least enjoyable part of the job.

Once the data is cleaned and standardized for practical use, data scientists mine it in search of patterns. During this process they refine algorithms and use their coding skills to build training sets for machine learning. These tasks require prolonged periods of concentration, working alone with minimal interruptions.

After performing an in-depth analysis, the data scientist discusses the findings with the client. Rather than presenting pages of data, most make their findings easier to understand by creating charts, graphs, and maps using data visualization tools such as Tableau and QlikView. As Gupta notes, "A picture is worth a million datasets. Data scientists . . . create presentations with an appropriate flow to narrate a story the data can tell in a way that is easily comprehensible and compelling to the stakeholders."[12]

Education and Training

Most data scientists have a master's degree in data science, computer science, data analytics, mathematics, or a related field. They are usually skilled programmers who write code to extract, manipulate, and update data using programming languages like Python, R, MATLAB, and SQL. Some create their own code using machine-learning algorithms. And around half of data scientists have a doctorate, which gives them the educational background necessary to work in fields like advanced robotics and artificial intelligence.

Students who hope to become data scientists can attend data science boot camps offered by many colleges and universities. These four- to six-month crash courses focus on coding, machine learning, data science, and other relevant topics. Students should also take as many math courses as they can and study database theory, database design, and operating systems like Windows and Linux.

Accreditation is not required to become a data scientist, but some seek certification to give them a competitive edge in the job market. The Data Science Council of America offers several types of accreditation for data scientists with different levels of experience. Microsoft offers advanced accreditation called MCSE: Data Management and Analytics Certification.

Skills and Personality

Data scientists are highly organized people with skills in mathematics and analytics. They have strong powers of concentration, an eye for detail, and the ability to work alone with mind-bending piles of data day after day.

Data scientists need a good understanding of science, according to Scott Beliveau, chief technology officer at the US Patent and Trademark Office. "A data scientist really is a scientist at heart," he says. "But rather than using chemicals or other things, a data scientist uses data—numbers, zeros, sometimes it's textual information—to try and solve and answer problems."[13]

Solving problems is only part of the job. Data scientists need good business sense to understand commerce and problems faced by small businesses and corporations. Data scientists also need to work efficiently in a business environment. They participate in company meetings and are required to explain their complex data analyses to engineers, marketers, operations managers, chief executive officers, and others. This means they must communicate clearly and in plain language so all can understand. Data scientist Karen Church writes, "Great data scientists can bridge the gap between technical and nontechnical stakeholders, ensuring that everyone is on the same page, communicating methods and results in a transparent and understandable way which helps ensure the work [has the desired impact]."[14]

Working Conditions

Most data scientists work full time in an office. Some work as freelancers in home office settings. They spend long hours sitting at desks and might work overtime when deadlines loom. While the work is often difficult, the job search website Glassdoor names data scientist as one of the top jobs in America every year. Data scientists are said to have high levels of job satisfaction.

Employers and Earnings

Data scientists are in great demand in every economic sector and at companies that range from independent start-ups to multinational corporations. There is a shortage of professionals in this field, and the dire need for data scientists translates into higher salaries. The Bureau of Labor Statistics (BLS) says the median annual pay for data scientists in 2023 was $108,020. Those

Searching for Data Treasure

"A data scientist's day is more than just code and data; it's a continuous exploration of the vast data wilderness, where they not only uncover hidden treasures but also shape the narrative of industries and societies. With every challenge they conquer, every insight they unearth, and every problem they solve, data scientists play a pivotal role in shaping the data-driven future. So, whether you're an aspiring data scientist or simply curious about the magic behind the data curtain, remember that each day in the life of a data scientist is a testament to the power of data and the boundless potential it holds for innovation and progress."

—Ashish Gulati, data science consultant

Ashish Gulati, "A Day in the Life of a Data Scientist," KnowledgeHut, January 24, 2024. www.knowledgehut.com.

who work in scientific research industries earned an average of $126,430. However, in 2024 Glassdoor said the average data scientist salary offered in job postings was $157,000, with a high of $190,000. Whatever the average figure, data scientists are some of the best-paid professionals in the country.

Future Outlook

The global demand for data scientists has rapidly increased in recent years. The BLS says that employment of data scientists is expected to grow by 35 percent through 2032, much faster than the average for all occupations. Data scientists' skills are needed in the burgeoning fields of cybersecurity and cloud computing, and technological innovations such as quantum computing and artificial intelligence will speed up their work yet also make it more important that the scientists are there to interpret the results.

Find Out More

Association for Computing Machinery (ACM)

www.acm.org

The ACM is a professional organization for data scientists, computing educators, and researchers. The association has over eight hundred local chapters worldwide that are open to students and professionals. The ACM website offers educational resources for students, including tech talks, journals, and research papers.

Data Science for Social Good

www.datascienceforsocialgood.org

Data scientist Chris Holdgraf launched this organization to make the world a better place by using data science. The website offers educational materials such as tutorials, summer fellowships, and information about the community projects it sponsors.

National Center for Women & Information Technology (NCWIT)

https://ncwit.org

This organization works to increase the participation of girls and women in computer science fields. The NCWIT focuses on students and offers a wide range of educational resources, including videos, blogs, and a newsletter.

Mathematician

What Does a Mathematician Do?

In 2020 Daniel Larsen was obsessed with trying to find a solution to a complex mathematical problem involving numbers known as Carmichael numbers. These are not prime numbers but entities known as pseudoprimes; they are composed of three prime numbers multiplied together. Carmichael numbers were first identified more than a century ago, and since then, mathematicians have been searching for a formula to easily identify them in long strings of numbers.

In 2022 Larsen devised such a formula. When he wrote out the solution, the intricate process filled twenty-six pages. At the time, Larsen was a seventeen-year-old high school student. He entered his work in the Regeneron Science Talent Search and won a $100,000 prize. Larsen also sent his work to mathematician Carl Pomerance, who had written a paper about Carmichael numbers in 1994. According to Pomerance, "[Larsen's] proof is really quite advanced. It would be a paper that any mathematician would be really proud to have written. And here's a high school kid writing it."[15]

In 2024 Larsen was a math major at the Massachusetts Institute of Technology. Like many mathematicians,

A Few Facts

Typical Earnings
Median annual pay of $116,440 in 2023

Educational Requirements
Bachelor's degree in mathematics, master's degree or doctorate preferred by most employers

Personal Qualities
Puzzle solver, math lover, analytical, good communicator

Work Settings
Full time in office settings, some travel

Future Outlook
Growth of 30 percent through 2032

A Demanding and Rewarding Passion

"Math is a tiring thing. When dealing with mathematics, especially research, you repeatedly think about the same thing. Understanding the math someone else has conducted and presented isn't always easy. Articles are usually relatively short, but you must constantly think and analyze what you read. . . . At times you will struggle, get exhausted. . . . Sometimes, I will toss the problem aside and forget it for months. But sometimes, when I get lucky, or the inspiration fairy comes along, I will get an idea or a new thought. Then I will take up the problem again and easily solve it."

—Ali, mathematician

Ali, "Why I Became a Mathematician," Medium, January 10, 2023. www.ali.medium.com.

Larsen sees beauty in math. "I've been drawn to understanding how things work, what the fundamental structure and order of something is, and math is full of these beautiful pictures of how seemingly unrelated concepts are part of the same idea," says Larsen. "You have these beautiful connections. There's a great sense of harmony and unity."[16]

The beautiful connections made by mathematicians form the foundation of the modern world. Math professionals generally work in one of two fields, theoretical mathematics or applied mathematics. Those who work in theoretical mathematics search for breakthroughs, like Larsen's, that can help advance mathematical knowledge. Theoretical mathematicians develop mathematical theories using numerical concepts such as integers, real numbers, rational numbers, complex numbers, and infinite cardinal numbers. When they have a breakthrough, they will write and publish an article and present it to others in mathematical journals or at conferences.

Applied mathematics, on the other hand, is concerned with solving practical problems in business, science, technology, engineering, and more. Applied mathematicians work with geometry, linear algebra, game theory, computational mathematics, and other types of math. Some work in software development, designing and implementing mathematical models used for algorithms that provide commands to computers. Mathematicians who work in the finance industry use math concepts such as statistics, probability theory, and stochastic [involving a random variable] calculus to analyze markets, assess risk, and improve stock trading strategies. Some mathematicians work in the field of operations research. They use mathematical modeling and optimization methods to help companies improve efficiency, reduce costs, and manage logistics, supply chains, and transportation.

A Typical Workday

Most mathematicians have extremely complex duties, which can vary depending on their employer. They might spend many hours analyzing data and developing formulas that can be used in real-world projects such as improving artificial intelligence (AI) software for an online retailer. Time might be dedicated to studying statistics and computational methods and designing encryption systems. Mathematician Brittany Craig specializes in quantum communications, overseeing a team of engineers and scientists who perform experiments with optical equipment. "It's so hard to describe what I do in a day because it's always so different," Craig says. "The gist of it is that I spend my time in a lab working with lasers and testing radio frequency communications and reading up on other work being done in the quantum field."[17]

Those who spend their days on pure research need to stay well informed about the latest developments in their field. This means studying mathematical journals and holding seminars with others in their profession. Mathematicians who work for colleges and universities teach courses while working on research projects. Describing his work life, mathematics professor John Baez writes, "[I] spend a lot of time travelling, giving lectures, going to conferences, talking to people, or just working in interesting places. . . . I also spend a lot of time blogging, mainly explaining math and physics. Explaining things is a great way to clarify one's ideas, especially if you demand of yourself that your explanations be as clear as possible, with as little jargon as possible."[18]

Education and Training

Some mathematicians have only a bachelor's degree in mathematics, which qualifies them to work for many government agencies. However, most employers who hire mathematicians require advanced degrees, either a master of science in math or a doctorate in math.

High school students who hope to become mathematicians need to take as many math courses as possible, including geometry, algebra, statistics, and calculus. Since most math professionals also create data analysis software, students should become proficient coders familiar with programming languages such as Arduino IDE, Python, and C or C++.

Prospective mathematicians should consider attending summer enrichment programs in math, commonly referred to as math camps. These programs try to make math fun; campers create apps, work on puzzles, participate in competitions, meet professionals in the field, and even build robots. Summer enrichment programs are often hosted by colleges and universities and can be found in most states. The American Mathematical Society website features a detailed list of residential programs nationwide. In addition to boosting their learning, those who participate in math summer camps show that they are motivated students who have an interest in academics. This can enhance their chances of attending the college of their choice.

College students studying for a bachelor's degree in mathematics take advanced math courses in differential equations and linear and abstract algebra. Most educational institutions require students to take related courses in computer science, engineering, or physics. Postgraduate students obtain degrees in theoretical or applied mathematics. Math master's degree programs involve courses in real analysis, complex analysis, probability, scientific computing, and differential equations. Students learn through a combination of lectures and seminars and spend time working independently to solve problems. Those who pursue a doctoral degree in mathematics immerse themselves in extremely complex subjects, including the theory of mathematics, mathematical logic, statistical and mathematical analysis, topology, and stochastic processes.

Skills and Personality

Mathematics can be mind-bogglingly complex. But at its most basic, math is about solving puzzles, and most mathematicians love tackling problems. This requires extremely strong analytical skills. Math professionals spend their days combing through massive amounts of data. They need to remember the smallest details to form analytical opinions. Mathematicians also need highly developed coding skills, since they often write customized software programs to develop new techniques and models.

Like most professionals, mathematicians need to be able to explain their work in plain language to associates, including engineers, scientists, business and marketing managers, and others who may be less proficient in math. Mathematician Rami Luisto emphasizes the importance of developing good communications skills: "You don't need to be a superb orator, but [you need to] discuss complicated topics with people who are not in your own small research group bubble. Most of the jobs require you working as a part of a team, and teams tend to work [poorly] if the information is not flowing."[19]

Working Conditions

Theoretical mathematicians often work alone when searching for answers to big problems. Those who work in this field estimate they spend around 30 percent of their time reading through professional journals, talking to other mathematicians, and attending conferences. Applied mathematicians usually have full-time jobs in offices, research centers, and classrooms. But it is commonly said that mathematicians can only concentrate on a task for about three hours before they need a break from the mental gymnastics of the job. Perhaps this is why tech companies and other employers often allow mathematicians to set their own schedules and work from home.

Employers and Earnings

Theoretical mathematicians often work at colleges and universities, where they teach math to future scientists and engineers. Theoretical math professors also study pure mathematics, relying on grants to fund ongoing research. Some theoretical mathematicians work in high-end research centers like the CERN particle physics laboratory in Switzerland or the Jet Propulsion Laboratory in Pasadena, California.

Applied mathematicians work in many economic sectors, including finance, insurance, online retail, automotive, social media, gaming, and robotics. Therefore, financial analyst and advisor, investment banker, mechanical engineer, statistician, computer programmer, and robotics engineer are all positions that mathematicians might pursue. Various government agencies hire mathematicians to conduct research related to

Designing Games with Numbers

"A love affair with numbers would serve me well in my chosen field of game design. . . . If a game designer needs to explain how something will work to a computer programmer, then using mathematical equations is one of the best ways. If a game design has to be passed along to a second game designer, then finding mathematical equations in the documentation is such a relief. . . . Mathematics allows you to express the relationships between sets of numbers in a very precise manner. And for game designers, it's best to be precise because the job requires you to know which numbers to use."

—Sande Chen, game designer

Sande Chen, "Reflections on Mathematics in Game Design," Game Developer, January 23, 2020. www.gamedeveloper.com.

climate change, cryptology, weapons development, and intelligence gathering.

The Bureau of Labor Statistics (BLS) says the median annual wage for mathematicians was $116,440 in 2023. Those who worked in the science and tech sectors, including research and development for AI and robotics, earned a higher median salary of $139,670.

Future Outlook

Mathematicians are in high demand across a wide range of industries. According to the BLS, employment for mathematicians is expected to grow by 30 percent through 2032, much faster than the average for all occupations. The largest demand for math professionals will come from the communications and medical manufacturing industries. Many schools and universities are investing heavily in STEM subjects to ensure that students are prepared to meet the demand.

Find Out More

American Mathematical Society (AMS)

www.ams.org

The AMS represents mathematicians, researchers, and educators. It promotes mathematics research through the publication of books, journals, and blogs and sponsors programs for student education. The society's website lists information about math summer camps in nearly every state.

Mathematical Association of America (MAA)

https://maa.org

The MAA is an international community of mathematicians, computer scientists, STEM professionals, students, and teachers. The association hosts competitions, provides curriculum resources, and offers student resources, including problem-solving books and information about regional conferences.

Society for Industrial and Applied Mathematics (SIAM)

www.siam.org

This organization is dedicated to advancing the application of mathematics. Its website provides information about educational programs, student SIAM chapters, upcoming conferences, publications, and research.

Economist

What Does an Economist Do?

Paul Krugman is a Nobel Prize–winning economist, author of more than twenty books, and a columnist for the *New York Times*. Like most economists, Krugman makes regular predictions about the strength of the economy. He provides readers with information about price inflation, interest rates, the national debt, and other complex financial issues. But Krugman says economics is not just about money. "Money may come into it. It's not about corporations. It's about people. It's about what people do," he says. "But it's about a fairly limited set of things that people do. . . . It's about buying and spending and making a living."[20]

Krugman explains that in economic terms, people are rather predictable. As an example, he cites farmers who are motivated to produce food in order to earn a profit. The same profit motive encourages truck drivers to transport the food to warehouses and owners of supermarkets to sell the food. Consumers go to work to earn money to buy the food. As Krugman says, no one tells these people to behave in this way, but their behavior forms the basis of economics. "We count upon people being predictable," he says. "If we're asking what a million people are going

A Few Facts

Typical Earnings
Median annual pay of $115,730 in 2023

Educational Requirements
Master's degree in economics

Personal Qualities
Analytical, good math and reading skills, independent thinker, detail oriented

Work Settings
Full time in offices

Future Outlook
Growth of 6 percent through 2032

Nobel Prize–winning economist Paul Krugman (pictured) makes predictions about the strength of the economy. In their work, Krugman and other economists consider many math-based factors, including price inflation, interest rates, and the national debt.

to do, then on average, they're going to be predictable enough that we can build our lives on that predictability."[21]

Some economists study microeconomics. This includes the financial decisions made by individual consumers and small businesses exemplified by Krugman's farmers and truck drivers. Another major field of study is known as macroeconomics. This branch of economics focuses on large-scale financial factors, such as international trade, national productivity, and interest rates (the amount a lender, like a bank or credit card company, charges a borrower for the use of money). Those who specialize in macroeconomics rely heavily on complex mathematical formulas to make predictions about issues that affect manufacturing, trade, and all facets of society. Macroeconomists create statistical models to study economic data, forecast trends, and interpret the behavior of financial markets. Macroeconomists consider the costs of education, health care, energy, and goods and services. They study unemployment figures, worker productivity statistics, and wages.

Some economists work for the US central banking system, called the Federal Reserve, widely referred to as the Fed. These economists analyze transactions at commercial banks, retail outlets, stock markets, trading companies, and many other markets. They coordinate with banks in foreign countries, including China, the United Kingdom, and Japan, to monitor international trade.

The most closely followed work by economists at the Fed concerns the raising and lowering of interest rates. Economists at the Fed crunch numbers, create graphs, and write reports about bank holdings, consumer prices, and other financial indicators. The insights of the economists might prompt the Fed to lower interest rates, which helps the economy grow faster, as people and businesses can borrow money at lower interest. A fast-growing economy might cause inflation, in which the price of goods and services rises quickly. When inflation hits, economists might recommend that the Fed raise interest rates, which helps lower prices by slowing economic growth. Macroeconomist Amy Fontinelle puts these complex concepts in perspective:

> Economics is like a giant puzzle that seeks to understand how people navigate a world with limited time, money, and resources. At its core, economics revolves around the concept of scarcity which means there's never enough of everything to go around. This scarcity forces us to make choices about what to produce, how to produce it, and who gets to consume it. Economists study these choices through various lenses.[22]

A Typical Workday

The work life of economists depends on their field of specialization, their education level, and the length of their career. Economists who work in the public sector spend their days analyzing government policies, budgets, and financial data produced by various agencies. Government economists provide Congress with information that predicts how raising or lowering taxes will impact government and society. These economists spend their days making graphs using software such as Microsoft Excel. The graphs are used in presentations to explain economic concepts and provide forecasts to banking officials, government workers, and others.

Economist Bryane Michael says more-experienced economists might work for corporations or public policy institutes known as think tanks. He explains, "They will do . . . statistical work. Much of their writing is for internal use only, and often politely accepted (and then ignored). Many will draft more authoritative sounding briefs, internal memos and will often advise their colleagues. . . . They usually do a lot less Excel and graph making, and will focus their time on SPSS [econometric software]. They may also spend time publishing policy [briefs]."[23]

Economists who are professors at colleges and universities balance their teaching duties with research. They spend time devising or refining economic theories by building mathematical models and testing data. The goal is to have the work published in professional journals and books. Academic economists travel to conferences, where they present their ideas and engage in debate with colleagues over theoretical math concepts. Some take on side work as business consultants.

Private sector economists work for banks, businesses, and investment firms. Fontinelle provides an example of work performed by an economist at Apple: "Say you're interested in better understanding how the latest iPhone may be received by consumers if it [is] priced $100 higher or $200 higher than the latest

Helping People Live Their Best Life

"Economists see the bigger picture of a society and its behavior. They determine the value of your money, they determine the amount of interest you will be charged on your home loan, how much tax to be collected and the list keeps going. They basically control each and every resource aspect of your life. They can literally manipulate the value of your life if they want to. But most of us don't. . . . The whole idea of the subject is to help people to be more satisfied than before, to help them to be happy and make sure they are living a life they dreamed of."

—Anaparthy Charan, economics student

Anaparthy Charan, "What Is It Like to Be an Economist?," Quora, 2024. www.quora.com.

release. An economist that works for Apple may decipher macroeconomic information to better understand how a consumer may react to a higher or lower price."[24]

Michael refers to economists who are at the top of the profession as guru economists. There are only a few of these experts. They are in demand at exclusive conferences like the World Economic Forum held in Davos, Switzerland, where they give speeches and present complex economic theories to high-ranking government officials and business leaders. Some, such as Krugman, write for major publications and provide comprehensive economic forecasts that are monitored by financial industry insiders and leading politicians.

Education and Training

Harvard University economics professor Greg Mankiw has advice for an aspiring economist: "Take as many math and statistics courses as you can stomach."[25] These courses include calculus,

Clarifying the Data

"I spend a lot of my day searching for and collecting relevant data. Without data, you will be very constrained as an economic consultant, so it's a given that I spend so much time on this task. Data management, processing and analysis are also key elements I focus on during most days. As an economist, it's important to be able to clearly communicate the findings of data, which basically means drafting reports highlighting the most relevant results obtained. Clients rely on us to provide clarity from complexity!"

—Robin Lechtenfeld, economist, Cambridge Econometrics

Robin Lechtenfeld, "Spotlight on Robin Lechtenfeld," Cambridge Econometrics, September 13, 2022. www.camecon.com.

linear algebra, real analysis, probability theory, mathematical statistics, and game theory.

While most economists have a master's degree, those who wish to work for local or state governments can find work with only a bachelor of arts degree in economics. Students working toward this degree study economic theory, macroeconomics, international economics, and economic growth and development. Some focus on obtaining a bachelor of science degree in economics. This course of study focuses on mathematics and statistics. Students research economic theories aimed at solving real-world problems in business, health care, the environment, and other sectors.

A bachelor of science in economics provides the strongest foundation for graduate-level study. Most job postings for economists require a master's degree in economics, data analytics, mathematics, business, finance, or accounting. Those pursuing master's degrees take courses in forensic accounting, financial statement analysis, advanced corporate finance, and data-driven decision-making.

A PhD in economics is necessary for those who wish to work at the Fed, the US Department of the Treasury, the World Bank, and most think tanks and international agencies. Those working toward a PhD write dissertations on subjects such as macroeconomics, microeconomics, labor economics, and industrial organization.

After obtaining a degree, some economists seek certification, which can lead to better job opportunities and higher salaries. The National Association for Business Economics offers professional certification as a Certified Business Economist to those with at least a four-year degree and two years of work experience.

Skills and Personality

Economists need strong analytical skills to scrutinize dense theoretical papers and large datasets concerning financial, social, political, and scientific issues. They are able to think in abstract terms about how various financial indicators will affect the buying decisions of millions of people. Economists rely on their mathematics skills to create economic models. They need computer skills to analyze data and create charts and graphs. And economists should be able to clearly communicate their complex big-picture ideas in basic terms that clients, colleagues, and average citizens can understand.

As Krugman says, human behavior is the key to understanding economics. Economists with a good understanding of social sciences like consumer psychology, history, and sociology can make more informed financial predictions. And most successful economists are independent thinkers who develop unique insights and theories that attract attention at conferences, seminars, and classroom lectures.

Working Conditions

Economists work full time in offices, where they collaborate with financial professionals including data scientists and statisticians.

Those who are employed by the government generally work very little overtime. Economists in academia might work longer hours when engaged in research projects. And they often travel to conferences and seminars.

Employers and Earnings

Economists work for government agencies, banks and investment firms, international organizations, and think tanks. Some work in the media, explaining economic concepts to the public in articles, blogs, and podcasts. The Bureau of Labor Statistics (BLS) says the median annual wage for economists in 2023 was $115,730. Those who worked for firms conducting scientific research and development earned $140,940, while economists in local government positions earned $91,980 on average.

Future Outlook

Modern society is based on money, and economists are needed to make forecasts about sales, market trends, and employment. Additionally, the government depends on economists to handle complex issues related to taxes, spending, and banking regulations. The BLS says these trends mean that employment of economists is expected to grow by 6 percent through 2032, slightly faster than the 4 percent predicted for all jobs.

Find Out More

Agricultural & Applied Economics Association
www.aaea.org

This nonprofit organization focuses on the economics of farming and food production. The association offers mentorship programs and hosts symposiums, workshops, and an annual conference.

American Economic Association (AEA)

www.aeaweb.org

The guiding principle of the AEA is providing knowledge about economics to students, teachers, professionals, and the public. The association offers career information for high schoolers and resources including seminars, economic literature, and lists of graduate school programs.

National Association for Business Economics (NABE)

www.nabe.com

The NABE is the premier organization for economists in the private sector. The association has a strong focus on education and provides scholarships, certification, and information about careers.

Computer Information and Research Scientist

What Does a Computer Information and Research Scientist Do?

The tech world is moving rapidly, and the media is filled with stories about the social and cultural impact of artificial intelligence (AI), machine learning, robotics, blockchain technology, and quantum computing. The chatbot app ChatGPT began making news almost immediately when it was released in late 2022. ChatGPT, which uses AI chiefly to create logically structured written texts in response to prompts, had been downloaded more than 110 million times by mid-2024. This made ChatGPT the fastest-growing software application in history. Artificial intelligence is also behind the latest innovations in robotics, while blockchain technology is the force driving the cryptocurrency boom. Meanwhile, the development of quantum computers holds the promise of revolutionizing the digital world in ways that are not yet understood.

There has been a great public debate about the pros and cons of AI, blockchain, robots, and other advanced tech. But there has been little discussion about the computer and information research scientists who go to work every day to create this

---

A Few Facts

Typical Earnings
Median annual pay of $145,080 in 2023

Educational Requirements
Master's degree

Personal Qualities
Technical knowledge, analytical skills, good communicator, business knowledge

Work Settings
Full time in offices

Future Outlook
Growth of 23 percent through 2032

next-generation technology. Depending on their job, these professionals might be referred to as computer scientists, information research scientists, applied scientists, or AI scientists.

Computer and information research scientists conduct in-depth research to help engineers design games and gaming hardware. Their work can be seen in navigation and guidance systems, smartphones, self-driving cars, and other products. Computer scientists who work in the entertainment industry are responsible for the AI programs that suggest music and movies to users of Netflix, Spotify, and other streaming services. Anyone who shops ecommerce sites interacts with the work of computer and information research scientists. They spend their days perfecting a website's ability to mine data, translate languages, analyze hardware and software performance, address customer complaints, prevent fraud, and improve core search functions.

Some of the most important work performed by computer and information research scientists involves writing, testing, and analyzing complex machine learning algorithms. Cybersecurity expert Wayne Archibald says this work is used to improve the way robots interact with the physical world: "Computer and information research scientists create the programs that control the robots. They work closely with engineers who focus on the hardware design of robots. Together, these workers test how well the robots do the tasks they were created to do, such as assemble cars or collect data on other planets."[26]

A Typical Workday

Computer and information research scientists spend much of their time reading, learning, and innovating. They might seek new ways of doing something by studying hardware and software manuals. Computer scientists read dissertations and academic research papers to learn about complex subjects such as logic,

The work of computer and information research scientists has contributed to the development of gaming hardware, navigation and guidance systems, smartphones, self-driving cars, and more. They also write, test, and analyze complex machine learning algorithms.

information theory, and topology (the properties of geometric objects). Researchers also consult older books and essays that cover traditional subjects, including philosophy, math, and physics. AI scientist Rik Koncel-Kedziorski says he spends 85 percent of his time at work learning and 15 percent innovating. He explains:

> The most important trait of an AI researcher is that they know a lot about AI research. Ideally, an AI researcher should have some breadth; that is, they should know at least something about a wide-ranging set of problems in multiple subdisciplines e.g. language, vision, robotics, time-series data, planning. . . . [Each day] I read at least one hard paper in detail, following references as needed to gain a deep understanding of the work. Hard papers for me are the ones that challenge my intuition about what

should work . . . or that take me a bit outside my field but are so impressive that I need to learn everything about what they're doing over there so I can replicate it over here.[27]

Computer and information research scientists often work with teams of other highly educated professionals. They share their findings with other scientists, electrical engineers, and computer hardware engineers to help them solve difficult problems. Some days are spent simplifying complex algorithms so they can be used in practical applications.

Those who hold a doctoral degree usually have a great amount of independence, as a research scientist with the handle Nefrpitou writes:

In research labs, with a PhD, you work on niche problems and often you have the freedom to pick which problem you want to solve, as long as it aligns broadly with the goals of your company or lab. . . . Once you choose a problem, you work on it for a year or two, maybe even longer if it's okay with your bosses. . . . During all this, you have freedom of project, and of time. You are your own boss, for the most part. You'd only have to update some key folks about your research once every quarter or so. It's a relaxed life, but you need to be self-motivated to solve the problem.[28]

Education and Training

Computer and information research scientists typically have degrees in computer engineering, software engineering, information systems, information technology, or a related field. While a bachelor's degree might be adequate for entry-level jobs in the field, most employers require information research scientists to have a master's degree in computer science, data science, or computer engineering. Those who wish to conduct pure research need a doctoral degree.

Becoming a computer and information research scientist is a long-term goal that requires education, experience, and determination. High school students who hope to work as computer research scientists one day should focus on math courses, including calculus, statistics, trigonometry, and algebra. Students should take physics, chemistry, and communications as well as computer science classes. Coding is central to a career as a computer and information research scientist, and students can learn important programming languages like R, Python, and SQL online. Working on computer hobby projects can also be beneficial to students.

Those pursuing a master's degree take courses in systems operations and management, programming, and software design and development. Students study linear algebra, optimization, neuroscience, cognitive science, algorithms, and the theory of computation. Master's programs also teach research, analytical, and leadership skills.

Undergraduates often enroll in internship programs in which they have an opportunity to observe professional computer and information research scientists at work. Interns gain valuable experience managing and troubleshooting problems with computers, software, robotics equipment, and other technology. Students working as interns expand their networks and connect with those who can provide references and job recommendations after graduation.

Skills and Personality

Computer and information research scientists need to have comprehensive technical knowledge of software and computer hardware like circuit boards, processors, chips, and other electronics. Scientists in this field rely on analytical skills to troubleshoot problems and find innovate ways to solve problems. They use logic

Learning as an Intern

"In my junior year of college, I had the opportunity to be an intern in the technology sector of a large bank. . . . [Through my internship] I learned that I'm personable and enjoy communication, partnerships, puzzles, and problem solving. . . . This helped me determine that I wanted to work hands-on with customers and help come up with technical solutions to their problems or goals. Internships and school projects are a great way to learn what part of the computer science industry you enjoy and remember; you don't have to like every computer science job out there to like computer science. Be open to different possibilities."

—Rebekah Lester, computer scientist

Rebekah Lester, "A Day in the Life of Computer Scientist Rebekah Lester," All Together, October 31, 2022. https://alltogether.swe.org.

and reasoning to identify the strengths and weaknesses of the solutions they devise.

Computer and information research scientists are often team leaders and thus need highly developed communications skills. They work with analysts, engineers, project managers, department heads, business managers, and vendors. They need to listen to coworkers and clearly present information and ideas to others.

Computer and information research scientists require business knowledge and a drive to accomplish goals. Their employers likely spend large sums of money on research, and the scientists need to show that their work has helped increase profits.

Working Conditions

Most computer and information research scientists work forty hours per week in offices, laboratories, and workshops. When major projects are nearing completion and deadlines are looming, they might work overtime, including nights and weekends.

New Math Concepts Every Week

"About once a week, I deep dive on a fundamental mathematical concept that I don't fully understand. These topics are farther afield from the typical math I use daily, but studying almost any math seems to make me smarter in complex and diffuse ways. And of course, whenever a conference happens, I am obliged to read as many of the new papers . . . as I can manage. You can never read too much in this exciting and interdisciplinary line of work!"

—Rik Koncel-Kedziorski, AI scientist

Rik Koncel-Kedziorski, "A Day in the Life of an AI Researcher," *Kensho Blog*, May 16, 2023. https://blog.kensho.com.

With the computer, software, and robotics industries changing very rapidly, computer and information research scientists regularly work to update their knowledge and skills. They take online courses and might even attend refresher college classes. Traveling to attend seminars is another aspect of the job. Conferences allow researchers to meet and socialize with other experts in their field. These connections can be very important when fresh ideas and suggestions are needed for particularly difficult projects.

Employers and Earnings

The Bureau of Labor Statistics (BLS) says 28 percent of computer and information research scientists work for the federal government. They might work in cybersecurity or hold top-secret clearances at the US Department of Defense, where they develop weapons systems. Other computer and information research scientists are employed in the tech and biotech industries and at engineering firms.

According to the BLS, the median annual salary for computer and information research scientists was $145,080 in 2023. Those who were employed in the software industry earned the highest pay, around $233,110. Research scientists who were employed by the federal government earned an average salary of $119,480.

Future Outlook

According to the BLS, computer and information research scientists are in high demand; employment for these professionals is expected to grow by 23 percent through 2032. And those who work as computer and information research scientists can expect to have a lasting influence on the world. As journalist Doug Wintemute writes, "[This field] greatly contributes to society, solving our biggest computing problems and improving our effectiveness and efficiency. These professionals impact our manufacturing, healthcare systems, finances, and businesses."[29]

Find Out More

Association for the Advancement of
Artificial Intelligence (AAAI)
https://aaai.org
The AAAI is a scientific society focused on pairing human intelligence with computers. Artificial intelligence is spreading into many fields, and the AAAI offers conferences, workshops, periodicals, and books on the structure, uses, and growth of AI. The society also provides student scholarships, grants, and other honors.

Computing Research Association (CRA)
https://cra.org
The CRA is dedicated to linking computer researchers from industry, academia, and government. The association has a strong focus on students, and its website provides information about research grants, awards programs, graduate school options, and career building.

IEEE Computer Society

www.computer.org

The IEEE Computer Society is dedicated to computer science and technology and provides information about networking and career development for educators, scientists, engineers, and students. Its website contains numerous educational and career-building resources, including online courses and books, webinars, scholarships, and certification preparation.

USENIX Association

www.usenix.org

USENIX is also known as the Advanced Computing Systems Association. It is a community of engineers, systems administrators, scientists, and technicians that hosts advanced computing conferences, promotes research, and shares information. The USENIX student section provides tech sessions and tutorials, grants, and information about student paper awards.

Physicist

What Does a Physicist Do?

Michio Kaku is a theoretical physicist. He is also an enthusiastic physics promoter who explains complex concepts in simple language to the general public on TV, radio, and the internet. Kaku says his enthusiasm comes naturally: "[Most physicists] from a fairly early age, are fascinated by the universe and its fantastic wonders. We want to be part of the romantic, exciting adventure to tease apart [the universe's] mysteries and understand the nature of physical reality. . . . We are more interested in black holes and the origin of the universe than with making tons of money."[30]

Physicists can be found studying the nature of physical reality in every branch of science. The experiments they perform and the theories they perfect provide a foundation for modern chemistry, biology, medicine, genetics, geology, and more. As physics professor Paul Bloom explains, "Physics is about understanding how nature works—how it does the things that it does—from the smallest scales of subatomic particles to the largest scales of the universe as a whole."[31]

Albert Einstein is undoubtedly the world's most famous physicist. Einstein developed theories about

A Few Facts

Typical Earnings
Median annual pay of $155,680 in 2023

Educational Requirements
PhD in physics

Personal Qualities
Curiosity; self-discipline; strong math, critical-thinking, and communication skills

Work Settings
Offices and laboratories

Future Outlook
Growth of 5 percent through 2032

light, atoms, time, space, gravity, and energy that changed modern science. Einstein published his most famous theories in the early twentieth century, but his work continues to inspire generations of physicists and scientists. Einstein's successors built on his original formulas to develop solar cells, televisions, lasers, nuclear power, and other amazing innovations.

Like Kaku, Einstein worked in theoretical physics. He employed mathematical models to develop theories that explained the interactions between matter and energy. These theories continue to help describe the workings of the universe. But theoretical physics is only one specialization in the field. Particle and nuclear physicists work at the smallest scale on the spectrum, studying the properties of atoms and subatomic particles such as quarks and electrons. Professionals known as quantum physicists conduct research into the behavior of atoms, electrons, and light particles called photons. Some quantum physicists spend their days working to perfect a new generation of fast-charging batteries that harvest and store energy from photons.

Computational physicists combine computer science, physics, and applied mathematics to solve extremely complex problems. They use algorithms, numerical analysis, and datasets to replicate physical processes and phenomena related to science, engineering, technology, economics, and medicine. Materials physicists study the physical properties of molecules, nanostructures, and rare compounds, while medical physicists focus on radiation therapies and developing the next generation of magnetic resonance imaging machines.

A Typical Workday

The workdays of physicists reflect their particular specialties, but most perform similar tasks. Physicists spend long hours reading and thinking to develop scientific theories that explain natural

The magenta spots in this NASA image show two black holes in the Circinus galaxy, located 13 million light-years from Earth. Black holes are just one of the mysteries of the universe that physicists study.

phenomena. Most stay current in their field by reading articles published on arXiv, an online physics archive.

Mathematics is the language of physics, and physicists spend hours writing out complex equations that provide others with precise explanations of their concepts. Some physicists test their theories working with teams that conduct experiments. Experimentation sometimes requires a physicist to write code for unique software programs or design new scientific equipment.

Physicists often rely on outside funding for their projects. They write proposals and hold meetings with those who provide research funds. Physicists also spend time writing research papers for publication in hopes of sharing their discoveries.

Education and Training

Most physicists have a PhD in physics or a related field. But Kaku says high school students who wish to pursue a career in physics

Pushing Boundaries at CERN

"Being a physicist at CERN [the European Organization for Nuclear Research in Geneva, Switzerland] is an exhilarating, mind-bending, and collaborative experience. Imagine yourself working at the forefront of scientific discovery, surrounded by brilliant minds from all over the world. You'd be collaborating on experiments that push the boundaries of our understanding of the universe, from the tiniest particles to the vast expanse of space. . . . [You are] part of a global community of researchers, sharing ideas, debating theories, and celebrating breakthroughs together. The atmosphere is intellectually stimulating, with a constant flow of conferences, seminars, and workshops."

—Mia James, physicist

Mia James, "What Is It Like to Work at CERN?," Quora, 2024. www.quora.com.

do not need to be as smart as Einstein. Students do need to be good at math, especially calculus, linear algebra, geometry, and statistics. And like Einstein, students should be driven by intense curiosity about the universe and humanity's place in it. Kaku says science projects are an excellent way to dive into the world of physics. And he recommends that high school students read books about famous physicists and contact those who work in the field. "Role models are extremely important," he says. "If you cannot talk to a real physicist, read biographies of the giants of physics, to understand their motivation, their career path, the milestones in their career. A role model can help you lay out a career path that is realistic and practical."[32]

For college students, it is necessary to first obtain a bachelor's degree in applied physics or in a related science or engineering field. Courses that provide a foundation for entering a graduate program in physics cover advanced calculus and essential physics subjects, including thermodynamics, Newtonian mechanics, magnetism, and electricity.

Students with a bachelor's degree in physics often enhance their knowledge by working as laboratory technicians or research assistants. Some apply for internships through organizations like the American Physical Society to gain hands-on experience. Performing internships and research assistant work improves a student's chances of getting into a graduate degree program.

Most universities offer a master of physics degree, but as Kaku writes, those who choose to pursue a doctorate select a field of specialization. "Within physics, there are many sub-disciplines you can choose from," he writes. "For example, there is solid state, condensed matter, low temperature, and laser physics, which have immediate applications in electronics and optics. My own field embraces elementary particle physics as well as general relativity."[33] Research-oriented PhD programs can take four to five years to complete. Essential doctoral courses include electrodynamics, classical mechanics, and quantum mechanics. Students conduct research in their area and write and publish a dissertation on their work.

Skills and Personality

Physicists often say they were extremely curious kids who were always asking others, "Why?" They might have taken apart their bicycle or dismantled computers to see how they functioned. This curiosity continues to drive them through their education and careers. A physicist who goes by the handle Bogfoot94 relates this story: "I wanted to know how things work and at some point my parents could no longer answer some of my questions, so during school I thought I'd learn everything I needed to know in order to understand the world and slowly I began to realize that the more I learned, the more questions I had, and the more questions I asked in school the fewer answers I'd get."[34]

Like other physicists, Bogfoot94 combined curiosity with the willingness to work hard. Physicists spend their days reading, studying, and experimenting while searching for answers. Physicists need self-discipline and strong critical-thinking skills to perform the challenging work associated with the field. Patience and excellent math skills are needed to test theories. When it comes time to explain their work to others, such as when they present ideas at conferences or write technical reports for publication, physicists need good communication skills.

Working Conditions

Physicists work in diverse settings, from classrooms and laboratories to particle accelerators and mission control rooms at the National Aeronautics and Space Administration (NASA). Most work forty-hour weeks, but at the culmination of major projects, physicists might work up to twenty hours a day. Some work off the clock, conducting research on nights and weekends when they believe a breakthrough is near.

Employers and Earnings

The Bureau of Labor Statistics (BLS) says that around 40 percent of physicists are working in either scientific research or scientific development. Scientific research institutions include laboratories funded by universities, such as the Argonne National Laboratory in Illinois, and those overseen by the federal government, including the US Department of Energy, the US Department of Defense, NASA, and the National Nuclear Security Administration. Some physicists work in high-end research centers like the CERN particle physics laboratory in Switzerland or the Jet Propulsion Laboratory in Pasadena.

Physicists who focus on scientific development might work for companies that are seeking to produce a new generation of products, from pharmaceuticals and electronics to automobiles and airplanes. Some go on to start their own companies. Two of

Exciting Internship at NASA

"I am currently a junior research assistant . . . in the Astrochemistry/Planetary Sciences Department [at NASA]. A normal day for me is spent manipulating and analyzing data obtained from the ALMA (Atacama Large Millimeter Array) Radio Observatory. Right now, I am observing Venus's atmosphere, using radio spectroscopy to identify chemicals, temperatures and wind speeds. . . . My favorite part of this internship is learning from the most brilliant people on the planet. The first half of my internship was in person at the NASA facility, so it was really exciting to meet some of the minds behind the amazing things NASA has been doing."

—Mark Castaneda, engineering physics major

Mark Castaneda, "Engineering Physics Major Mark Castaneda '25 Tells Us What It's Like to Intern at NASA," University of the Pacific, July 21, 2022. www.pacific.edu.

the richest people in the world, Elon Musk and Jeff Bezos, have backgrounds in physics.

Around 15 percent of physicists work at academic institutions, where they teach, conduct research on cutting-edge projects, and mentor students. Some physicists find work in the private sector, where they use their expertise to solve problems in technology, health care, and engineering.

The BLS says the median wage for physicists in 2023 was $155,680. Those who worked in scientific research and development services were earning $176,960. Those employed by the federal government earned an average wage of $135,300. Physicists working at colleges and universities were on the lower end of the pay scale, earning $87,840 on average annually.

Future Outlook

The BLS says employment for physicists will grow by 5 percent through 2032. As the fields of space exploration and scientific research continue to expand, physicists will remain in demand. The BLS warns, however, that most research funds are provided by the federal government, and budgetary concerns might limit growth in some fields.

Find Out More

American Astronomical Society (AAS)

aas.org

The AAS is made up of physicists, mathematicians, engineers, and others interested in promoting research and education in the astronomical sciences. The society offers educational grants, career advice, and leadership programs for students.

American Institute of Physics (AIP)

ww2.aip.org

This organization was founded to promote and advance the physical sciences. The AIP website offers publications, career resources, and information about student programs (including the Society for Physics Students) and graduate school programs.

American Physical Society (APS)

www.aps.org

The APS hosts scientific meetings, disseminates physics research findings, and advocates for physics education. The society works with teachers and schools to train the next generation of physicists and provides programs that offer career pathways to populations underrepresented in the sciences.

Source Notes

Introduction: The Language of the Universe

1. Iain Anderson et al., "Making a Major League Baseball Team with Math: An Interview with Tim Zue, Boston Red Sox," Mathematical Association of America, March 31, 2022. www.mathvalues.org.
2. Quoted in Mathnasium, "Math Improves English, Writing, History, Science, Music," October 22, 2021. www.mathnasium.com.
3. Quoted in Anne Marie Helmenstine, "Why Mathematics Is a Language," Mathnasium, September 26, 2020. www.mathnasium.com.

Accountant

4. Tracy Coenen, "Criminal Defense Work: Financial Crimes," Sequence Inc., 2024. www.sequenceinc.com.
5. Coenen, "Criminal Defense Work."
6. Quoted in Will Erstad, "Myth vs. Reality: What Is Being an Accountant Really Like?," Rasmussen University, June 3, 2019. www.rasmussen.edu.
7. Quoted in Ryan, "What Is an Accountant Day to Day Schedule Like?," Career Village, December 13, 2022. www.careervillage.org.
8. Quoted in Will Erstad, "Myth vs. Reality."

Data Scientist

9. Diogo Ferreira, "How Would You Explain the Job of a Data Scientist to a 5 Year Old Kid?," Quora, 2022. www.quora.com.
10. Quoted in *U.S. News & World Report*, "Data Scientist Overview," 2024. https://money.usnews.com.
11. Sakshi Gupta, "A Day in the Life of a Data Scientist: What to Expect," Springboard, July 1, 2023. www.springboard.com.
12. Gupta, "A Day in the Life of a Data Scientist."
13. Quoted in *U.S. News & World Report*, "Data Scientist Overview."
14. Karen Church, "The Most Underrated Skill in Data Science: Communication," Medium, July 25, 2023. https://medium.com.

Mathematician

15. Quoted in Jordana Cepelewicz, "Teenager Solves Stubborn Riddle About Prime Number Look-Alikes," *Quanta Magazine*, October 12, 2022. www.quantamagazine.org.
16. Quoted in Lili Wright, "The Ups and Downs of Daniel Larsen," *Indianapolis Monthly*, August 28, 2022. www.indianapolismonthly.com.

17. Quoted in Mandy Hay, "A Day in the Life: '16 Math and Applied Physics Grad Brittany Craig Speaks on Her Exciting Research," KatieCareer Virtual Center, St. Catherine University, 2024. https://katiecareervc.stkate.edu.
18. John Baez, "What's a Day Like in the Life of a Mathematician?," Quora, 2024. www.quora.com.
19. Rami Luisto, "Moving from Academia to Industry—a Mathematician's Tale," Rami Luisto, PhD, August 1, 2020. https://ramiluisto.medium.com.

Economist

20. Paul Krugman, "What Is Economics?," MasterClass, 2024. www.masterclass.com.
21. Krugman, "What Is Economics?"
22. Amy Fontinelle, "A Day in the Life of an Economist," Investopedia, November 4, 2023. www.investopedia.com.
23. Bryane Michael, "What Do Working Economists Do Day-to-Day?," American Economic Association, 2024. www.aeaweb.org.
24. Fontinelle, "A Day in the Life of an Economist."
25. Greg Mankiw, "Advice for Aspiring Economists," *Greg Mankiw's Blog*, May 23, 2006. https://gregmankiw.blogspot.com.

Computer Information and Research Scientist

26. Wayne Archibald, "What Does Computer or Information Research Scientist Do?," Career Village, February 11, 2023. www.careervillage.org.
27. Rik Koncel-Kedziorski, "A Day in the Life of an AI Researcher," *Kensho Blog*, May 16, 2023. https://blog.kensho.com.
28. Nefrpitou, "What Exactly Does a Computer Scientist (with a PhD or Masters) Work on, Compared to a Regular Software Engineer?," Reddit, 2021. www.reddit.com.
29. Doug Wintemute, "How to Become a Computer and Information Research Scientist," Best Colleges, December 23, 2022. www.bestcolleges.com.

Physicist

30. Michio Kaku, "So You Want to Become a Physicist?," Dr. Michio Kaku, 2024. https://mkaku.org.
31. Quoted in Lauren Ford, "What Do Physicists Do?," North Central College, January 29, 2021. www.northcentralcollege.edu.
32. Kaku, "So You Want to Become a Physicist?"
33. Kaku, "So You Want to Become a Physicist?"
34. Bogfoot94, "Why Did You Become a Physicist?", Reddit, 2021. www.reddit.com.

Interview with a Physicist

Nicole Yunger Halpern has been conducting physics research for thirteen years. She is a theoretical quantum physicist at the National Institute of Standards and Technology and an adjunct assistant professor at the University of Maryland. She conducted this interview with the author by email.

Q: Why did you become a physicist?
A: First, I grew up reading constantly, especially novels. I loved building worlds in my head, and now I do so for a job. Second, I've always loved learning about everything. Physics involves . . . perhaps not quite everything, but an awful lot. I use mathematics, computer science, and information theory; I collaborate with chemists and biologists; I have to know my history (for example, what did Albert Einstein say to Niels Bohr about the nature of quantum theory during the 1920s?); I mentor, write, and give presentations.

Q: What is your typical workday like?
A: I prefer to read shortly after waking up, to begin filling my mind. Ideally, I'll read a physics paper, to glean background information for a research project or to keep abreast of the latest discoveries. After breakfast, I form a to-do list for the day. I reserve mornings for my most difficult work: calculations, writing and editing papers, writing grant proposals, and responding to referee reports (part of the communal scientific dialogue about papers I'm working to publish). I eat lunch with my husband if I'm working at home and he isn't in a meeting; with the lunch group I run for researchers interested in thermodynamics (the science of energy), on Wednesdays; or while reading a publication by the American Physical Society, otherwise. I often check the arXiv—an online repository of brand-new physics papers—while finishing my tea.

Meetings, emails, administrative tasks, and preparations for upcoming presentations fill the afternoon. I take a break at the gym before dinner, then finish up stray tasks in the evening.

Q: What do you like most about your job?
A: The act of creation. I love building bridges between disparate disciplines; devising equations to describe a phenomenon that I observe or expect to observe; or creating a model.

Q: What do you like least about your job?
A: Applying for grants, writing institutional reports, serving on committees, etc. This work benefits the scientific community as a whole, and it helps ensure that my students and postdocs enjoy free time to wrestle with research problems directly. Still, I'd enjoy having more of that time myself.

Q: What personal qualities do you find most valuable for this type of work?
A: I'd top the list with diligence, self-discipline, and a commitment to continual learning. Research involves setback after setback and so requires perseverance. Don't worry if setbacks dispirit you, though; I've grown used to them, but they used to faze me more, as they faze many physics students. If you're such a student, find a trusty mentor who'll help you contextualize your experiences, and keep a log of your successes. Don't worry if you haven't learned a particular subject or technique as long as you're willing to work hard to acquire that knowledge. A strong background in mathematics helps, as do imagination and organizational skills. Finally, scientists—human beings—do science, so I value colleagues' respect for others and good-heartedness.

Q: What advice do you have for students who might be interested in this career?

A: Have fun! You might not enjoy every hour or every day—some integrals are simply frustrating—but physicists have the privilege of learning continually and exploring the ultimate nature of reality. What more of a treat could one ask for?

Q: What kinds of projects are you currently working on?

A: Everything I work on falls under the auspices of quantum physics, information theory, and/or thermodynamics—perhaps with a sprinkling of some discipline out of left field, such as biophysics or particle physics. At the moment, I'm working on useful autonomous quantum machines. Autonomous machines have grown ubiquitous, from Roomba vacuum machines to pizza-delivering drones. But these devices obey the classical mechanics and electrodynamics codified by the end of the 1800s. Certain quantum machines—such as quantum engines, refrigerators, and batteries—can outperform their classical counterparts according to certain metrics—for example, the average power with which batteries can charge. But running a quantum machine typically requires one to cool particles to near absolute zero and to perform tricky control operations. Autonomous quantum machines, which require relatively little control, have a better chance of earning their keep. I worked with collaborators on the first arguably useful autonomous quantum refrigerator, and we're now expanding that line of research.

Other Jobs If You Like Math

Accounting clerk
Actuary
Air traffic controller
Astronaut
Astronomer
Atmospheric scientist
Auditor
Banker
Bookkeeper
Cashier
Chef
Chemist
Claims adjuster
Cloud architect
Construction manager
Cost estimator
Database administrator
Data miner
Demographer
Educator

Electrical engineer
Electrician
Financial analyst
Forensic analyst
Geologist
Hospital administrator
Industrial engineer
Insurance underwriter
Logistician
Marketing research analyst
Mechanical engineer
Nurse
Operations research analyst
Pharmacist
Physician
Real estate agent
Sales representative
Statistician
Stockbroker
Surveyor

Editor's note: The online *Occupational Outlook Handbook* of the US Department of Labor's Bureau of Labor Statistics is an excellent source of information on jobs in hundreds of career fields, including many of those listed here. The *Occupational Outlook Handbook* may be accessed online at www.bls.gov/ooh.

Index

Note: Boldface page numbers indicate illustrations.

accountant, **8**
  education/training requirements, 7, 10–11
  employers of, 13
  future job outlook, 7, 14
  information on, 14
  role of, 7–9
  salary/earnings, 7, 13–14
  skills/personal qualities, 7, 11–13
  typical workday, 9–10
  work settings, 7
Accounting Today (website), 14
Agricultural & Applied Economics Association, 38
Allec, Logan, 12–13
American Astronomical Society (AAS), 56
American Economic Association (AEA), 39
American Institute of Certified Public Accountants (AICPA), 11, 14
American Institute of Physics (AIP), 56
American Mathematical Society (AMS), 26, 30
American Physical Society (APS), 56
Archibald, Wayne, 41
architect, 4
Argonne National Laboratory (IL), 54
artificial intelligence (AI), 40
Association for Computing Machinery (ACM), 22
Association for the Advancement of Artificial Intelligence (AAAI), 47
Association of Government Accountants (AGA), 11, 14

Baez, John, 26
Beliveau, Scott, 19–20
Bezos, Jeff, 55
Bjälkebring, Pär, 5
black holes, 49, **51**
blockchain technology, 40
Bloom, Paul, 49
Board of Accountancy, 9, 10
Bureau of Labor Statistics (BLS), 62
  on accountant, 13–14
  on computer information and research scientist, 46–47
  on data scientist, 20–21
  on demand/wages for math-related jobs, 5

on economist, 38
on mathematician, 29
on physicist, 54, 55

Carmichael numbers, 23
Castaneda, Mark, 55
CERN (European Organization for Nuclear Research, Switzerland), 28, 52, 54
certified public accountant (CPA), 7–8, 9, 13
  accreditation of, 10–11
Charan, Anaparthy, 35
ChatGPT (chatbot app), 40
Chen, Sande, 29
Church, Karen, 20
Coenen, Tracy, 7–8, 9
computational physicist, 50
computer information and research scientist, **42**
  education/training requirements, 40, 43–44
  employers of, 46
  future job outlook, 40, 47
  information on, 47–48
  role of, 40–41
  salary/earnings, 40, 46–47
  skills/personal qualities, 40, 44–45
  typical workday, 41–43
  working conditions, 45–46
  work settings, 40
Computing Research Association (CRA), 47
Craig, Brittany, 25
cryptocurrency, 40

Data Science Council of America, 19
Data Science for Social Good, 22
data scientist, **18**
  education/training requirements, 15, 19
  employers of, 20
  future job outlook, 15, 21
  information on, 22
  role of, 15–16
  salary/earnings, 15, 20–21
  skills/personal qualities, 15, 19–20
  typical workday, 17–18
  working conditions, 20
  work settings, 15

economist
  education/training requirements, 31, 35–37
  employers of, 38

future job outlook, 31, 38
information on, 38–39
role of, 31–33
salary/earnings, 31, 38
skills/personal qualities, 31, 37
typical workday, 34–35
working conditions, 37–38
work settings, 31
Einstein, Albert, 49–50

Federal Reserve, 33
Ferreira, Diogo, 15–16
Fontinelle, Amy, 33, 34–35

Galileo Galilei, 6
game designer, 29
Glassdoor (job search website), 20, 21
Gulati, Ashish, 21
Gupta, Sakshi, 17, 18

Hester, Alan, 10, 11
Holdgraf, Chris, 16

IEEE Computer Society, 48

Jet Propulsion Laboratory (Pasadena, CA), 28, 54

Kaku, Michio, 49, 50, 52
Koncel-Kedziorski, Rik, 42–43, 46
Krugman, Paul, 31–32, **32**, 35, 37

Larsen, Daniel, 23–24
Lechtenfeld, Robin, 36
Lester, Rebekah, 45
Luisto, Rami, 27–28

macroeconomics, 32–33
Mankiw, Greg, 35
material physicist, 50
Mathematical Association of America (MAA), 30
mathematician
education/training requirements, 23, 26–27
employers of, 28–29
future job outlook, 23, 29
information on, 30
role of, 23–25
salary/earnings, 23, 29
skills/personal qualities, 23, 27–28
typical workday, 25–26
working conditions, 28
work settings, 23
mathematics
applied, 24, 25

broad applications of, 6
demand/wages for jobs related to, 5
other jobs in, 62
theoretical, 24
medical physicist, 50
meteorologist, 4
Michael, Bryane, 34, 35
microeconomics, 32
Musk, Elon, 55

National Aeronautics and Space Administration (NASA), 55
National Association for Business Economics (NABE), 37, 39
National Center for Women & Information Technology (NCWIT), 22

Occupational Outlook Handbook (Bureau of Labor Statistics), 62

Peters, Ellen, 5
Peterson, Angela, 12
physician, 4–5
physicist
education/training requirements, 49, 51–53
employers of, 54–55
future job outlook, 49, 55–56
information on, 56
interview with, 59–61
role of, 49–50
salary/earnings, 49
skills/personal qualities, 49, 53–54
typical workday, 50–51
working conditions, 54
work settings, 49
Pomerance, Carl, 23
pseudoprimes, 23

quantum physicist, 50

Society for Industrial and Applied Mathematics (SIAM), 30
sports analyst, 4

theoretical physics, 50

U.S. News & World Report (magazine), 5
USENIX Association, 48

Watson, Ben, 9–10
Wintemute, Doug, 47
World Economic Forum (Davos, Switzerland), 35

Zue, Tim, 4